Contents

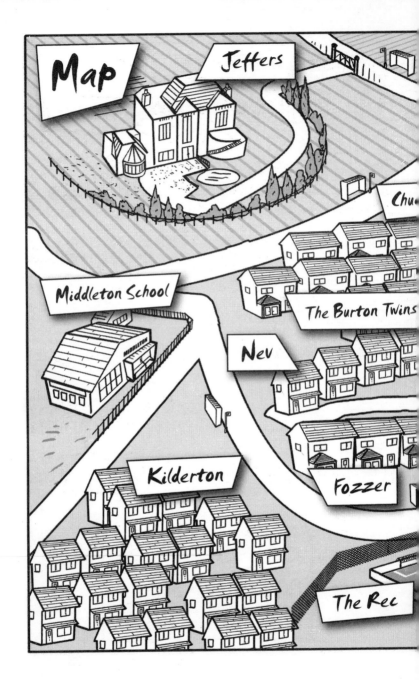

Meet the Jags

Name: Andrew Burton

Fact: He's the Jags' captain.

Loves: Spurs

FYI: The Jags may be his mates, but they'd better not forget he's the Skipper.

Andy

Burts

Name: Terry Burton

Fact: He's Andy's twin brother.

Loves: Football, football, and more football. He's football crazy!

FYI: He's a big Arsenal fan.

Dev

Name: Ryan Devlin

Fact: He's very forgetful.

Loves: Daydreaming!

FYI: He's always covered in mud and bruises.

Fozzer

Name: Hamed Foster

Fact: He can run like crazy, but he shoots like crazy too – sometimes at the wrong goal!

Loves: Telling bad jokes.

FYI: His best friend is Nev.

Keeps

Name: Jim Ward

Fact: He's the Jags' Number One goalie – whether he likes it or not!

Loves: Trying to score from his end of the pitch.

FYI: He's the tallest member of the Jags.

Jeffers

Name: Jeffrey Gilfoyle Chapman

Fact: He's the only one of the Jags who doesn't live on the Chudley Park estate.

Loves: Being in the Jags.

FYI: He's the Jags' top goal-scorer.

Name: Denton Neville

Fact: Nev is the Jags' most talented player.

Loves: Fozzer's bad jokes.

FYI: He keeps his feet on the ground and always looks out for his football crazy mates.

Name: Pam Burton

Fact: The Burton twins' mum, and a team 'mum' for all the Jags.

Loves: Sorting out her boys.

FYI: Doesn't actually like football!

Name: Jack Ward

Fact: He's Jim's dad and the Jags' coach!

Loves: Going on and on, doing his team talks.

FYI: He's taking his coaching exams.

The Magic of the Cup

My mate Fozzer knows more jokes than anybody. And he's always got an idea for something to do.
I didn't say his jokes or ideas were any good, though!

Fozzer   Nev, Nev. Why don't they build football grounds in outer space?

Nev   Because there wouldn't be any atmosphere. Fozzer. You told me that joke yesterday.

Fozzer   All right. What does Paul Ince eat at Christmas?

Nev   How do I know?

Fozzer   INCE pies, of course!

Nev   Fozzer, Fozzer. Wait a minute. You didn't just come round here to tell me jokes, did you?

Fozzer   No. Of course not. I can tell you jokes any time, can't I?

Nev Yeah. So what did you want to talk about? I'm trying to do that maths homework.

Fozzer Oh, it's much more important than that. Have you heard the draw for the Third Round of the Cup? It was on the radio when I got home.

Nev   No, who did we get? I still can't believe our own little Vale United have got to the Third Round of the FA Cup.

Fozzer   Well, get this! In the Third Round of the FA Cup, our own little Vale United have been drawn at home to Aston Villa of the Premier League. What do you think of that?

Nev   Aston Villa? At Valley Road?
No way, man!

Fozzer   It'll be great. All those big
Premier League stars, playing
against Frank Stubbins and
Danny Sprott.

Nev   Do you think they'll show
it on TV?

Fozzer Who cares? We've got to go to the game, haven't we? That's why I came round. I mean, they're the team that loves ice cream, right?

Nev Who are?

Fozzer Aston VANILLA, of course!

Full House

> *Everybody in Kilderton would want to see the game. So what chance did we have of getting tickets?*

Fozzer   Come on, Nev. Let's go down to the ground. If the tickets are on sale, we have to be first in the queue.

Nev   Being first in the queue is a
        good idea. But have you
        thought how we can pay
        for the tickets?

Fozzer I've got all my dinner money for
        next week and you've got the
        money you were saving up for
        new trainers. The tickets must be
        cheaper for kids. And it's only
        Vale United. They can't cost
        too much.

Nev   Yeah, but they're playing Villa. They'll put the prices up. United don't get many chances to make a bit of money.

Fozzer   I know. The manager was shaking the club cat up and down the other day, wasn't he?

Nev   Why? I didn't even know they had a club cat.

Fozzer   He wants to buy a new player and he was seeing if there's any money in the *kitty*. Ha, ha!

Nev   I wonder why there's nobody around? I thought there'd be lots of fans wanting to buy tickets.

Fozzer   I'll go and ask. You keep my place in the queue.

Nev   But there isn't a queue, man.

Fozzer   You never know. There might be
a rush in a minute.

Nev   Oh no, why the long face Fozzer? Don't tell me they've already sold out.

Fozzer   No. But they won't have tickets for another two weeks.

Nev   Well, that's okay. We can come back then, can't we?

Fozzer   Mmm. Maybe. But she said the tickets will be £20 each. How are we going to find £40 by then? That's no joke, is it?

Any Ideas?

The good thing about Fozzer is that he can't stay in a bad mood for long.

Fozzer   I've got it!

Nev   You've got what? Another joke?

Fozzer   Oh, I've always got another joke. What's black and white, black and white, black and white?

Nev   Um, a zebra crossing?

Fozzer No, man. A Newcastle fan
rolling down a hill. But I didn't
mean I've got another joke. I
meant I've got another idea for
how we can get those tickets.

Nev   Before you say anything,
Fozzer, I am not going to help
you rob a bank.

Fozzer   No, Nev, listen! Do you think the Jags are half as good as Vale United?

Nev   Well, we might be when we're grown up. But not yet, Fozzer. Not yet.

Fozzer   We must be half as good?

Nev   Okay, then. What if we are?

Fozzer   Why don't we charge people £1 to watch the Jags? If 40 people come, we'll have our £40!

Nev   But we never get 40 people watching one of our games.

Fozzer   That's because they don't know we're playing. We need to tell them. We can put posters up.

So Fozzer got some paper and pens to make posters. There was no stopping him.

Fozzer   Who are we playing next Sunday?

Nev   That team from Southdown. The Spiders.

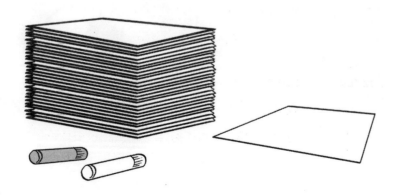

Fozzer Are we at home or are we playing them at WEB-ley Stadium?

Nev Fozzer, man. That's a really old joke.

Fozzer I know. I'm sorry. But look at this poster. What do you think?

Come and See the Stars of the Future!

Jags versus Spiders

The Vale

Kick-off
Sunday 11 a.m.

Only £1!

Standing Room Only

Well, it was a good idea. And it was a good match. The Jags won 2–1. But it didn't work out the way Fozzer had hoped.

Fozzer   I can't believe it! I spent so much time doing those posters!

Nev   Oh, I think the posters worked, Fozzer. I've never seen so many people at one of our games. It was great.

Fozzer   But what about our tickets? Why couldn't we charge £1 to watch the game? There must have been 40 people there.

Nev   Well, you heard what Mr Ward said. You can't charge people to watch boys playing a game in the park.

29

Fozzer   I *am* worried. The match is only three weeks away and £20 is a lot of money.

Nev   You heard what Mrs Burton said as well. All the Jags were playing. And all the Spiders too. It wouldn't have been fair for us two to keep all the money!

Fozzer   But it was *our* idea!

Nev   Yeah, but we *are* a team. What are we going to do? We'll just have to watch it on TV.

Fozzer   No. We *have* to be there. Look.
This idea is a winner, man.

Nev's Soccer School

at

The Rec

£5 per day

Nev   Nev's Soccer School? Gary
Neville? Phil Neville?

Fozzer No, DENTON Neville! You! You're the Jags' best player, aren't you?

Nev You want *me* to do a soccer school?

Fozzer Well, not on your own. I'll be there to get the money.

Nev   Fozzer, you're crazy. I love playing football but I'm not a coach, am I?

Fozzer   Not yet. But, hey, even Alex Ferguson had to start somewhere, didn't he?

Nev   Yeah, but he wasn't put in charge of Man United when he was ten years old.

Just the Job!

Well, Fozzer had run out of ideas for getting money to buy the tickets. The soccer school idea was never going to work. So why was he in such a good mood?

Fozzer   Nev! How's it going?

Nev   Not too bad. Shall we go to the Rec for a kick-around?

Fozzer   What's a goalie's favourite snack?

Nev   Um, beans on post. I saw that one in a comic yesterday.

Fozzer   Yeah. *My* comic. And I want it back. With all the football posters still in!

Nev   There you go. My mum won't
let me put any more pictures up
on my bedroom wall anyway.
She says they all fall down
when she opens the door.
Anyway, what about the game?

Fozzer   Don't you mean what about
the *big* game?

Nev   What about it? Have you got
another idea for getting some
tickets? They go on sale
tomorrow, you know.

Fozzer   Oh, we don't need tickets, man.

Nev   We'll never be able to sneak in.
There will be nowhere to sit.

Fozzer   How about sitting on the touchline? Haven't you seen the local newspaper?

Nev   Um, no. But Mum's got it indoors.

Fozzer   Come on, then.

Nev   Where am I meant to be looking?

Fozzer   Right there! Where it says "Joyful Jags!"

JOYFUL JAGS!

Jack Ward, Vale United's kit man, has found a Premier League team of ball-boys for the big Cup match at Valley Road next weekend.

Nev What? Does it mean that *we* are going to be the ball-boys? *The Jags* as ball-boys at the big match? WOW!

Fozzer The super Jags! Mr Ward says we'll be the best ball-boys ever. We've got to go to a special training session tomorrow after school!

Nev   I can't believe it! No wonder he told you not to worry about tickets! Just watch. The Jags are going to show everybody a thing or two about teamwork at the big match next week!

VALE UNITED 1
ASTON VILLA 4

The big day came. We sat right by the pitch, ready to get the ball when it went out. The players looked so big and so fast!

Burts   Hey, Nev! Look at him go!

Nev   Now he's got to get it across. A goal for Villa! United only lasted five minutes.

Fozzer   Come on United! You can come back!

Nev   You were right, Fozzer. Frank Stubbins has got it back to 1–1. What a shot! The crowd is going mad!

Fozzer   I know. But Villa have got the ball back already. Oh, no. That's 2–1 to Villa.

Our boys played really well. But Aston Villa were too good for us. They won 4–1. That's why they're in the Premier League.

Fozzer   What a game! What a day!

Nev   Yeah. United were unlucky, man.

Fozzer   *I* wasn't, though. Look! I got all these autographs as they came off the pitch!

Up for the Cup

The FA Cup is the oldest cup tournament in the world. It started in 1872. The Cup is different from the League. If you lose a game, you are out until next season. That is why Cup games are so exciting. The winner takes all!

The FA Cup Final at Wembley is one of the best days in football. About 90,000 fans go to watch at Wembley, all dressed in their team's colours. Millions of people watch it on TV, all over the world.

 One of the best things about the FA Cup is that little clubs get the chance to play against the big clubs. Usually the big club wins. But sometimes the little club wins. That's called an "upset" or a "shock". And everybody loves it when that happens. Except the fans of the big club!

 Who do you think will win the FA Cup this year?

Cup Quiz

Questions

1 When was the first FA Cup Final?

2 Where is the FA Cup Final played?

3 How many fans go to the Final?

4 What happens if you lose a game in the FA Cup tournament?

Answers

1 1872.

2 Wembley.

3 About 90,000.

4 You go out of the tournament until next season.

About the Author

Tom Watt, who wrote The Jags, is a big fan of the FA Cup. Some people say that's because he saw the very first FA Cup Final. That's not true. He may be old but he's not that old! He did write a big book about the history of Wembley, though. It was called *The Greatest Stage*.

In the old days, if the Final was a draw, they would play the match again. Now, they have extra time and a penalty shoot-out. Sometimes Tom and his son pretend that they are in the FA Cup Final and have a penalty shoot-out. Tom always loses!

THE JAGS

RISING★STARS

The Jags books are available from most book sellers.
For mail order information
please call Rising Stars on 0871 47 23 01 0
or visit www.risingstars-uk.com